pretty pink death scene

Sarah Marchant

BookLeaf Publishing

India | USA | UK

Presentation by *BookLeaf Publishing*

Web: www.bookleafpub.com

E-mail: info@bookleafpub.com

ISBN: 9789358315233

First edition 2023

found footage

camera eye clicks
shuttering the scene into frame

darkness curling around the edges
forging an uneasy alliance

i was a witch every year
and you had a black cat

our mothers brought us to church
in little purple dresses

we never stopped to question
the hand of fate

never asked our friend, the oracle,
how to change the color of the curtains

never wondered why the hymns
why the exultations

but we kept singing, small hands
tapping at piano keys

we built the altar to our bond
and burnt the sacrifice

as the prophet foretold
we would forever be intertwined

haunted house

there are ghosts in the walls of your split-level
house
watching as you paint my face garish colors
with too much mascara, performing
transformative rituals
preparing for a parade of imaginary suitors
making daydream lists and pursing my lips just
so:
the audience can see the haunting, can hear
the banging of cabinets and rustling of bedsheets
and the spirits follow us on that overnight
getaway
decadent chocolate and quiet panic attacks:
underneath the feminine script you are a savage
the foreshadowing evident from the start
specters invading your wiring and insulation
skulking behind clothes in your closet:
what had been only thick ink on notebook paper
spirals into stacks of typewritten pages
curated tomes to slice my softness apart:
you say the final incantation and time freezes
the crystal ball breaks
my heart is a shattered mirror
only offering ego death
and seven years of bad luck

until the sun comes up
until the flashbulb goes off
until the EMF meter lights up
and everything is revealed

creature feature

5

so the story goes
the smell of summer lingered in the air
grass dewy and the world shockingly green

my body bruised from field hockey
your voice booming across the landscape
neither of us knowing that god
wasn't too keen to answer our prayers

it took years of patience
to marry the earth
instead of obsessing
over the heavens

when the last fireside tale had been told
and the embers softened down to smoke
we climbed into those rickety bunks
your eyes still alight with flames

& you pushed me into the pool
mouth filling with water
chlorine up my nose
choking on grievances but

i cannot repent for something i did not do

& i'm crawling through this swamp
knees muddied
unpicking myself from your alligator teeth
skin striped with blood
immune to your crocodile tears

yelling timber as my heart stops

female revenge

Poor little Cinderella
tortured by her stepsisters
Go cry about it
See if the songbirds will save you
Shredding up dresses in changing rooms
with my talon-sharp nails
pink fabric pooling on the floor
My blade looks so good against your cheek

I'll bind you in thorns while she
spins around you like a ballerina
wrapping you up in ribbons
Our secret smiles give nothing away

Our signatures are surrounded by
drawings of hearts and stars
and silly inside jokes
you keep tripping on like landmines

Our characters appear in the credits
bold and underlined while you
petition for the starring role

You were never a princess
just a lowly acolyte

trailing behind the wrong god
Tell me, where is he now?
It seems he likes to watch you suffer

technology horror

my green globe is a halo hovering over my head.
your gray a set of devil horns sprouting.

never been able to pursue honesty because
it threatens to unravel fabric that's
already so loosely woven. pulling the
petals off roses. dissolving into
pixels. a psyche projected
through emails and status updates.

my happiness is a scar, wound reopening
with every crackle of the internet connection.

my limbs are sewn together
with wires, my savior
a low quality jpeg.

cursor floating through space.
hands hushed at the keyboard.
mouth flattened by graphic design.
posture bent & agonized.
punishing paragraphs sent to the printer
over & over, but every page
comes out blank.
staring silently ahead until
the screen goes dark.

exploitation

and you looked as me as if
i'd betrayed you with a kiss

sinking into dormitory carpet
like movie quicksand

i've tried to write this feeling away
stanzas about radio broadcasts
temptation shrouded in metaphors

but i've drained the cheap pens dry
and shorn down every crayon

don't concern yourself with tallying my sins
i've already collected too many to count

i'm sorry i ate of the forbidden fruit
it was just so red and so sweet
juice still sticky on my fingers

i'm sorry for indulging in
the miracle of her mouth
partaking in the communion
between her thighs

if i must be exiled from paradise
the brimstone will keep me warm
lost in the hellfire of her touch

you cannot uproot the poison from my soul
just as i cannot revive your cold, bloodless heart

ghost story

you want to be worshiped
my faith undying
your sainthood sacrilege

you desire a bouquet of blood
my servitude unyielding
your palms unclean

you crave violence
my teeth gritted
your fangs bared

it's not real i tell myself
repeatedly but i can still
feel your hands in my hair
tugging at the strands
our love is lethal but i
believe it must be universal
that everything needs to
hurt me to hold me tight
and your hologram still sings
its battle songs while i'm
trying to sleep wistful and
angry i'm waving my white flag
but the music keeps playing

and the choir is standing
from their seats to harmonize
and the cacophony is crashing
down on me how can you want
to part the waters while still
the ghosts of dead egyptians
shout their final pleas in
the dreadful, godless waves

low budget

Yeah, I've talked about you in therapy.
What more is there to say?

I guess plenty, but my memories
have an archival quality to them,
so some scenes are spotty
and the director keeps swapping the title cards
because he can't decide who is the lead.

But I am a poet, wisps of you threaded
through the narrative of each page,
and you are a novelist,
crafting a claws-out confrontation
in the middle of a diner.

I am a pianist, fingers flying
between black and white
to experiment with noise,
and you are a vocalist, crowing
to anyone who will listen
how I was the villain all along.

blood & guts

break my heart like a man
i am the sacrament
i am your tireless devotion

cover my fresh body with snow
have a cup of tea with my corpse

isn't this what you wanted

isn't this what i deserve
for my wicked, wicked ways

there's a hole in my chest
still warm
melting the slush away

leave me frozen in time
i'm a crime scene

your murder victim, tagged & bagged
ready for the flashlights
of cops, prepared for police sirens

i'm just another jane doe
features gouged to nothing

witchcraft

apologies for stealing your man
but maybe i wanted you instead
my jealousy like jolene
coveting your collection of freckles
because honestly he's embarrassing
and truthfully you can't spell for shit
but i wanna hold your hand
is that bad?
trying to earn your forgiveness
to get you underneath me
sharing the strawberry hookah
like a secondhand kiss
all blush & sugar
all movement in the dark
playing hypnotist
until i perfect my rituals
to enchant your mind
& ensnare your body
reciting the stanzas
that would make us legendary
the ceremony was almost complete
when our witnesses fled
at the end of the night
we were alone, shivering
it wasn't wise but i wanted
you to run away with me

home invasion

while i was asleep, you were unassuming
taking a dip into my nightmares to see
what was useful
but you don't deploy the full extent
of my frailty: just enough

don't plot against my inner sanctum
unless you bring a knife
you vampire
don't cross my threshold unwelcome

orange hair against pale skin
glimmering under the porchlight
i know what you are

with every step
the lightning strikes
sparking your path

mistress of cruelty
speaking my name like a curse
you dare to brand me bitch

and what are you
if not a work

of fiction?
your tongue in my mouth

your metal
carving through my chest
tracing my pulse

your oxygen
pulled from my veins
struck comatose

but i've taught myself
to walk insomniatic
your traps not catching

perform the exorcism
sever the soul from my flesh
but this won't be the last time i shriek
like a woman possessed

splatter

the twelve dancing princesses
plucking silver from a thicket of trees

the swing dancer, the scientist
the mother, the fuck-up

so sorry i met you
with malicious intent

the hiker, the botanist
the author, the performer

terribly sorry i daydreamed about
your demise on every page

the smoker, the porcelain doll
the psychologist, the zealot

dreadfully sorry for imagining
all the ways a girl can bleed

southern gothic

When I approached your legacy home,
a vulture was picking at a carcass
the dead grass, and your three child-
ren were guarding the front door.
Each of them looks a little like you
and a little like something I have
never seen before. Blonde and
angelic and unsettling. It must be
nice to bake the bread, scrub the
walls and floors, make everything
shine with holy light. The Lord's army
of miniature yous following every
step, chirping for milk like baby birds.
From the incestuous relations of
summer camps past to the "barefoot
and pregnant" of present day. Don't
you want to escape? Maybe not,
because the baby is crying and the
homestead needs tending and the
prison of your small town is rattling
the cage. The ivy grows so rapidly
you can't keep up as it covers every
window. Your clippers dull, your vision
narrows to a hazy point in the middle
distance. Other selves singing in choirs

and directing stage plays and saving
sparrows with broken wings. While your
one life – your precious, incomparable
life – crumbles brick by brick,
rotting at the foundation.

body horror

all the polite girls
with their vegan diets
and their surface-level feminism
gather in polite living rooms

while i sit in the corner
quietly imploding
my mind mutating

you're planning your wedding?
that's cool, did you know
i'm actually insane?

open wounds blooming
i'm a liar and a cheat
and mentally ill

it's been close to a decade
of feeling less than human

they're busy ascending the corporate ladder
while i'm stuck down in the mineshaft
parasites wriggling in my brain

far from romantic
i'm a threat to the cause

of polite girls in polite living rooms
discussing their polite challenges

as the galaxies corrode

science fiction

do the experiment
see what sticks

plug my arms with circuitry
all your solutions neon green

i'll be your homoerotic subtext, baby
if you promise to wipe the blood from my lips

your best clothes ruined for me
your smile a sign of terror

as the surgery commences
you'll see my insides have decayed

i've churned through so many iterations of
myself
you might not even know me anymore

you don't know me anymore
all you've met are clones

it's not my fault you decided
to go off-script, all cues improvised

why would it be me
who decides your fate

study the gospel text
like a secondhand dictionary

meet me in the morgue after midnight
clutch me tightly in the shadows

bizarro

Maybe they were rummaging for scraps
like hungry dogs.

Maybe when you fucked my friend you meant to
say
I'll only text you when he's in my bed.

Maybe when you kissed me your brain was
whirring
someday I'll meet a man and have his babies.

Maybe choosing a guy over me was like
choosing a honeybee over a hornet.

my sting bites venom into your bones
my syrup too bitter to swallow

watch me stalk my prey
watch me devour your dreams

sorry
watch me fall through the sky

scream queen

i will claw my way out of the ground
pushing through rain-wet soil
to reach you

i will talk my voice hoarse
scream my throat raw
until the rescue helicopter comes

i will drink the pig's blood
down to the last rusty drop
to keep your prom dress clean

i will pronounce the incantation
repeating the lines flawlessly
until my mirror face speaks latin

i will download the demon files
document their fiendish ways
until they break free

i will become you
in the final act
to get the glory

i will smother you with a pillow

holding so steady
until your protests cease

what an arrogant antagonist
what a gorgeous martyr
what a pretty pink death scene

death game

you were my friend
when i was a freak
unwanted in life
unmourned in death

we were an entity
beckoned by our name

which one of us
survived rape
a sink full of knives
starvation, famine and flood
every biblical plague

my sister in christ

now you can decorate my casket
the scent of funeral flowers
filling the windowless room

and the ticker counts down

congratulations
you've won

folklore

In the beginning, before the initiation of time
and space, before the invention of color when
the world was desaturated into grayscale, the
hues soaked into black and white,

our timelines were synchronized, right down to
our first names and taste in immature men.

Before the heavens and the earth were created,
before the firmament of sky and sea were set
into place,

there was us. Just us. The template.

In your short story, the best friend has long,
brunette hair and a class ring.

In your novel, the best friend is anorexic. She
always writes with a gel pen. Dolphins are her
favorite animal. She loves bands and movies that
you can't stand.

In your series, she
is a traitor.

Is history repeating for us? Do you love me?

How long until your paragraphs turn into prose?
Do you intend to slam the library of my failings
over my head? Will you book-bind all of my
insecurities with your deft fingers?

Will you decide New York is better for your
bones? Maybe Santa Fe?

Whatever the case, I'm here, battle-beaten and
bruised. Knuckles swollen, teeth grinding, jaw
clenched.

You're the sugar in my coffee, you're the
cyanide in my medicine. The problem and the
solution. The shackles and the skeleton key.

Don't leave me or my pretty little pill bottle
behind.

Please don't leave me here, alone and stranded.

apocalypse

The day everything ended
was in middle school
when a mean girl lied
to both of us about the other.
It was in high school
when we made the same connection
in different ways. Or maybe
it was on your wedding day
when I was your maid of honor
but she was the apple of your eye.

The real last day, when buildings collapsed
and I had to climb from the wreckage,
was 2015, when you'd had enough
of my morals. When no amount
of books or shared history
or familiar geography could save us.

Come into the museum of us.
See the sanctuary walls
shaking as the ground ruptures.
View the paintings of past indiscretions,
study the religious murals as every depiction
splinters and cracks.
Fracturing our temple.
Consuming our fragrant offerings.

Now, with only a pane of glass
between us, I am on display.
I am your exhibit.

Learn from me.
Heed my warnings.
If you follow to the letter,
you might make it out alive.

The day everything ended
I flicked my cigarette
into the gasoline-soaked structure
and watched the flames roar.

final girl

they will only give you more screen time
if your hair is blonde
if your eyebrows are perfectly shaped
if your tits are big enough
they will try to capture you
like a wild rabbit

but joke's on them because
i have the hidden knife
i have the blender that will
bash their skulls in
turn their brains into just another
mess on the kitchen floor

& and i am feral, untested, untamed
my immortality apparent

all the religion in all the world
couldn't redeem me

wedding invites and family christmas photos
clutter the front of the fridge
swarmed by my shortcomings
bitten by desire
baptize me in red, red wine

i'll let the alien reside in my chest
i'll let the romance last until tuesday

but don't expect me to go gently

blood trickles from a gash in my forehead
my tattoos punctuated by cuts & scrapes

these days i would need a spirit board
to ever speak with you again

i sucked the air right from your lungs
& you're dead to me

9 789358 315233